ENGLISH NURSES PRE-INTERMEDIATE LEVEL

Book 1

By Virginia Allum

ISBN 978-1-291-91990-5

90000

CONTENTS

1 Talking about blood pressure
2 Talking about movement
3 Talking about pneumonia
4 Talking about breast reconstruction
5 Talking about pain
6 Talking about infection control
7 Talking about conjunctivitis
8 Talking about depression
9 Talking about lung cancer
10 Talking about dysphagia

Unit 1: Talking about blood pressure

blood pressure
pulse
high
low
slow
fast
normal
pain
painkillers

**Activity 1: <u>Underline</u> the stressed part of the following words.
The first one is done for you.**
1.   <u>blood</u> <u>press</u> - ure
2.   pulse
3.   nor - mal
4.   pain – kill - ers

Activity 2: Watch the video at
<u>www.youtube.com/watch?v=qbU7Po63vPk</u> **and answer the
questions.**
1. What does the nurse want to do?
a   take Mr Browning's temperature
b   take some blood
c   take Mr Browning's blood pressure and pulse.

2. What is the problem with the patient's blood pressure?
a   It's too low.
b   It's a bit high.
c   It's very high.

3. What is the patient's pulse like?

a It's normal.

b It's too slow.

c It's faster than usual.

4. Why does the nurse think his blood pressure is a bit high?

a He might have a cold.

b He might need a rest.

c He might be in pain.

5. What will the painkillers probably do?

a They might make his blood pressure go down.

b They might make him feel better.

c They might bring his temperature down.

Activity 3: Listen again and write the correct words. Use the words in the box to help you.

some	higher	should	faster	take

Nurse: Hello, Mr Browning. Can I (1)_____ your blood pressure and pulse, please?

Patient: Oh, hello nurse. Yes sure.

Nurse: Mm. Your blood pressure's a bit (2) _____ than this morning. And your pulse is faster than usual.

Patient: Oh, are they? Why is that?

Nurse: If you are in pain, your blood pressure will go up and your pulse will get (3) _____.

Patient: Yes, I'm in quite a bit of pain at the moment.

Nurse: I'll get you (4) _____ painkillers. Then your blood pressure (5) _____ go down and your pulse should get slower too.

Patient: I see. Thanks for explaining it to me.

Activity 4: Put the phrases in the correct order.
a)   faster than usual
b)   take your blood pressure and pulse
c)   get you some painkillers
d)   blood pressure go down and pulse slower
e)   in pain, your blood pressure will go up
f)   bit higher than this morning

Activity 5: Match the beginning with the ending.
Watch the video again to check your answers.

1. Can I take	**a)** a bit higher than this morning.
2. Your blood pressure's	**b)** your blood pressure will go up.
3. And your pulse is	**c)** should go down.
4. If you are in pain,	**d)** your blood pressure and pulse, please?
5. Then your blood pressure	**e)** faster than usual.

Activity 6: Make a short conversation between a nurse and a patient. Use the prompts to help you. Role play the conversation; swap roles to practise both parts.

Nurse: Can / take / blood pressure / pulse, please?
Patient: Oh / hello / sure.
Nurse: Your blood pressure's / bit higher / this morning. pulse faster / usual.
Patient: Oh, are they? Why is that?
Nurse: If you / pain, your blood pressure / go up / your pulse / get faster.
Patient: Yes / I'm / quite a bit / pain / at / moment.
Nurse: I'll get / some painkillers. Then / blood pressure / should go down and / pulse should get slower too.
Patient: I see / Thanks / explaining it / me.

Grammar check: take and do
We use 'take' and 'do' in a lot of expressions describing things nurses do.
For example: *take a blood pressure,*
           do a dressing.

Activity 7: Put the following expressions together using *take* and *do*:

1. _____ your pulse.
2. _____ an ECG. (electrocardiogram, EKG)
3. _____ your temperature.
4. _____ some blood.
5. _____ a urine test.

Electrocardiogram

In the USA it is known as an EKG

In the UK / Australia/New Zealand it is known as an ECG

Unit 2: Talking about movement

Check that you know these phrasal verbs
lean back
lean forward
lie down
lift up
put down
sit down
sit up
stand against
stand behind
stand up
stand up facing me
turn around

Activity 1: Opposites

Match the opposite movements. The first one is done for you.

1.	lean forward	a)	sit down
2.	lift up	b)	turn around
3.	sit up	c)	lean back
4.	stand up	d)	stand in front of
5.	stand up facing me	e)	lie down
6.	stand behind	f)	put down

Asking 'Can you ...?'
Remember that after 'can' you write the verb without 'to'.
For example,
Can you stand up? Yes, I can stand up.
Can you turn around? Yes, I can turn around.

Activity 2: Write the instructions under the pictures. The first one is done for you.

stand up	lift up	lie down
sit up	stand behind	sit down

1. Can you lie down?

2. Can you _____?

3. Can you _____?

4. Can you _____ the walking frame?

5. Can you _____ on the wheelchair?

6. Can you _____ your leg?

Activity 3: Watch the video at
www.youtube.com/watch?v=dvPnQkRCEk8 **and answer the questions.**

1. Nurse Hannah asks the patient to _____ first?
a lie down
b sit up
c talk

2. Next, Nurse Hannah asks the patient to _____ facing her.
a lean
b sit down
c stand up

3. The patient says she finds it difficult to _____.
a walk
b talk
c sit

4. The patient should try not to _____ or she may fall.
a lean forward
b lean back
c stand

5. The last thing the patient does is to _____.
a lie down
b turn over
c sit down

Activity 4: Write the correct words to make the dialogue.

Nurse: Can you (1) _____ for me? OK that's right. Now can you stand up facing me?

Patient: I'll try.

Nurse: That's good. Can you (2) _____ towards me?

Patient: It's a bit difficult.

Nurse: OK Try not to (3) _____ back. You might fall if you lean back.

Patient: Oh. OK.

Nurse: Can you (4) _____ around now? That's it. Try to sit down on the chair now.

Patient: Can I sit now? I won't (5) _____?

Nurse: Yes. You can sit now.

Activity 5: With a partner, make a dialogue between a nurse and a patient. Use these phrases:
Can you ......,please?
Can you .... for me?
Try to .....

Use verbs of movement: sit down, stand up, lie down,
                fall, turn around, lean towards

13

Unit 3: Talking about Pneumonia

Check that you know these terms:
breathe in
breathe out
cough
hay fever
oxygen
phlegm
respirations
sneeze
specimen jar
sputum

Also, these expressions:
have a cough
I've got a cough
I keep coughing
I keep sneezing
I've got hay fever
bring up phlegm
Are you bringing up any phlegm?

Activity 1: Look at the diagram of the lungs and complete the information which follows.

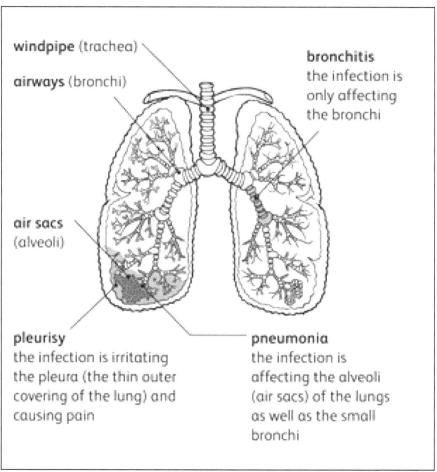

windpipe (trachea)

airways (bronchi)

air sacs
(alveoli)

bronchitis
the infection is
only affecting
the bronchi

pleurisy
the infection is irritating
the pleura (the thin outer
covering of the lung) and
causing pain

pneumonia
the infection is
affecting the alveoli
(air sacs) of the lungs
as well as the small
bronchi

From: <u>www.blf.org.uk/DynamicImages/a0820b96-0ae2-4735-9764- a067018516d0/Pneumonia_diagram.jpg</u>

There are three types of lung infections:
Bronchitis is the inflammation of the (1) _____. The bronchi

are the airways which lead off the trachea. Pleurisy is an infection

of the pleura. The pleura is a membrane which covers each

(2) _____. The pain in pleurisy is called a *pleural rub*. The

prefix 'pleuro' means *side of the body or rib*. Pneumonia is an

infection which causes the (3) _____ to fill up with liquid.

This makes it very difficult to breathe.

**Activity 2:Match the terms with their correct answers. The first
one is done for you.**

1. breathe in	a) air that goes into your body
2. breathe out	b) a gas we breathe from the air
3. breath	c) take air into the body
4. oxygen	d) clean jar that collects a small part of the body e.g. fluid
5. respirations	e) let air leave the body
6. specimen jar	f) breaths in and out

All about respirations

Noun	Verb
a cough	to cough / to cough up
a sneeze sneezing	to sneeze
phlegm sputum	to have a lot of phlegm / sputum not to have any phlegm / sputum
Hint: Remember to pronounce *gh* in *cough* as *f*	

Activity 3: Write the words to complete the meanings of the words.

sneezing	sputum	sneeze	phlegm	cough

1. When you have a _____, sputum comes up from your lungs.

2. If you cough up green _____, you may have an infection.

3. If you _____, liquid comes out of your nose.

4. We write 'atishoo' when we explain that a person is _____.

5. Sputum is also called _____ by some people.

Activity 4: Watch the video at
www.youtube.com/watch?v=ToSy0-Ycm2g and answer the
questions about the video. Select the correct answer.

1. How long has the patient had a cough?
a She's had it for over a week.
b She's having it for over a week.
c She's have it for over a week.

2. What does the nurse ask the patient to do?
a She asks to cough into a specimen jar.
b She asks her to cough into a specimen jar.
c She asks her cough into a specimen jar.

3. What does the nurse give the patient so it is easier to breathe?
a   She gives her an oxygen mask.
b   She gives her some oxygen.
c   She gives her a specimen jar.

4. What does the nurse give the patient to help with the pain?
a   She gives her an injection.
b   She gives her an infection.
c   She gives her some tablets.

Activity 5: Write the correct form to make the dialogue.

Nurse: How long have you _____ the cough? (have)

Patient: Oh, I've had it for over a week now. I _____ awful. (feel)

Nurse: Can you please _____ into this specimen jar? (cough)

Patient: I'll _____. (cough cough) There you are! Yuk.

　　　　It's green. (try)

Nurse: I'll give you some oxygen to make it easier to _____. (breathe)

Patient: Thank you. It is difficult.

Nurse: I'll _____ you some tablets to help with the pain. (give)

Patient: Thank you. My chest _____ a lot. (hurt)

Unit 4: Breast Reconstruction

Check that you know these terms
areola
breast
comfortable
heal
infection
nipple
numb / numbness
reconstruction
scar
sports bra
upright

Activity 1:   Underline the stressed part of these words. The first one is done for you.

1.   ar – e – <u>o</u> - la

2.   breast

3.   com – fort - able

4.   in – fec - tion

5.   nip - ple

6.   numb - ness

7.   re – con –struc -tion

8.   up -right

Activity 2: Label the picture of a breast. Match the number on the picture with the correct word. The first one is done for you.

1	a) areola
2	b) fat lobules
3	c) chest wall
4	d) skin
5	e) fatty tissue
6	f) nipple
7	g) chest muscle
8	h) milk ducts

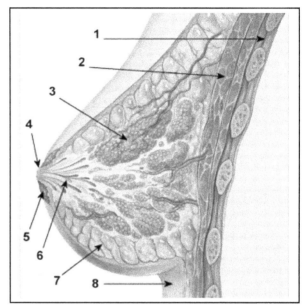

Medical terms: Do you know these medical prefixes and suffixes?

The two prefixes which mean 'breast' are 'mammo' and 'masto'

Activity 3: Write the correct words in these sentences.

numb   upright   scar   heals   sports bra

1. A cut _____ when it gets better.
2. A ____ is a raised mark on your skin which is left after a wound heals.
3. A part of your body feels _____ if you can't feel it.
4. A _____ is a type of underwear which supports your breasts well when you exercise.
5.   If you sleep_____, you sleep in a sitting position.

Nursing Focus: Asking for consent
Before you touch a patient you must ask for consent. This means asking for permission.
There are three types of consent:
1. Implied consent – This is where patients give you the idea that they are happy for you to touch them. For example, a patient may hold his arm out as you come near to show that it is OK to take his blood pressure. There is no need to say anything at all.

2. Verbal consent – You need to ask permission using a short phrase e.g. 'Is it OK if I take your temperature now?' Answer - 'That's OK', 'Yes, fine' or 'Sure'.

3. Written consent – This is often necessary under law. The patient usually signs a consent form to say they give permission e.g. for an operation, for a medical study, for a MRI.

Activity 4: Watch the video on youtube.
The nurse asks Mrs Song for consent before she talks to her about her operation. What does she say?

Nurse: Hello, Mrs Song. I'm going to explain what will happen after your breast reconstruction.
(a) All right?
(b) Is that all right with you?
(c) Is that OK?

Activity 5: Answer the questions about the video. Watch the video again to check your answers.
1. What operation is Mrs Song going to have tomorrow?
a) a breast removal
b) a breast reconstruction
c) breast development

2. After the operation the nurse will check Mrs Song's breasts ___.
a) every hour for the first 4 hours
b) every hour for 24 hours
c) 4 times an hour

3. Mrs Song's breasts may be a bit _____ after the operation.
a) sore
b) painful
c) numb

4. What does Mrs Song have to wear after the operation?
a) a hospital gown
b) a sports bra
c) a large bra

5. It will be better for Mrs Song if she sleeps _____ at first.
a) on her side
b) lying down
c) sitting up

6. Mrs Song is worried about getting _____?
a) numbness
b) an infection
c) scars

Activity 6: Match the beginnings with the endings.

1. I'm going to explain	a) around your nipples.
2. We'll check your breasts	b) sleep upright.
3. You may have numbness	c) signs of infection.
4. You need to wear	d) what will happen.
5. Make sure that you	e) your new sports bra.
6. Watch for any	f) every hour for the first four hours.

Giving advice: These expressions give advice to a patient:
1. You need to + verb

2. Make sure that you + verb

3. Watch for any + noun

Activity 7: Complete the dialogue using the phrases below.
a) you must phone the doctor
b) We need to check the blood supply
c) It's important to wear
d) Your nipples may feel a little numb
e) we'll check your breasts hourly
f) You should sleep up on three pillows

Nurse: I'm going to explain what will happen after your breast reconstruction. Is that OK?
Patient: Oh, thank you

Nurse: After your operation (1) _____ for the first four hours.
Patient: I see. Why is that?

Nurse: (2) _____ to your breasts.
Patient: I understand.

Nurse: (3) _____ after the surgery. Try not to worry about this as it is quite normal.
Patient: How long will the numbness last?

Nurse: Sometimes it takes a few months for normal sensation to return.
Patient: OK, so I don't have to do anything about it?

Nurse: No, you just have to wait until it goes away, I'm afraid.
(4) _____ your new sports bra day and night for the first week. Then you can just wear it during the day.
Patient: So, just to be sure, I wear the bra all the time for a week then only during the day.

Nurse: That's correct. **(5)** _____ for the first week as well.
Patient: Do you mean as if I am sitting up in bed?

Nurse: That's right. You should find that it is more comfortable as well.
Patient: What about scars? I don't want to get any scars on my breasts.

Nurse: If you do the exercises I showed you it is unlikely that you will have any scarring. The last thing I wanted to discuss with you is about infection. You will have to keep an eye out for any signs of infection in your breasts. If you notice any redness around the nipple or any discharge from the nipple, **(6)** _____.
Patient: All right, I'll make sure that I do that.

Activity 8: Put the six phrases from activity 7 under the correct headings. Which phrases are used to explain what will happen and which phrases give advice?

What will happen?	What should the patient do?

Unit 5: Talking about pain

Check that you know these terms:
ache /I've got a lot of aches./ It aches a lot.
analgesia / painkillers
capsule / suppository / tablet
drug chart
It hurts a lot
injection
PCA / patient controlled analgesia
pain / I'm in pain. / It's painful
pain scale / rate your pain

Describing pain
There are several different ways to describe pain.

1. **Pain**
* usually means a sharp pain e.g. 'I've got a pain in my stomach / hip / knee.'
* makes compound words e.g. back pain, shoulder pain, hip pain
* You say: It's very painful.

2. **Ache**
* usually means a dull pain
* makes compound words e.g. toothache, stomach ache, earache, headache
* a fixed expression **'aches and pains'** e.g. I've got a lot of aches and pains

3. **It hurts**
* general ache or pain e.g. My toe hurts a lot.

Activity 1: Complete these sentences using the verbs below.

painful   back pain   hurts
aches   sharp   stomach ache

1. I fell over. My knee _____a lot now.

2. I have arthritis. My knee _____a bit in the mornings.

3. I have an infected toe. It's very _____ especially when I stand up.

4. I think I ate something that was bad. Now I have a bad
_____.

5. I had a car accident last year. Most of the time I have severe
_____ and my hip aches a lot.

6. I get a _____ pain in my right shoulder when I try to lift my arm.

Read the text and complete activity 2:
Pain scales
There are three main pain scales that are used by patients to tell nurses about their pain. These are:
• PIPP or Premature Infant Pain Profile - nurses look at the expression on the baby's face and whether the baby is crying.
• Wong-Baker Faces – this scale is often used by children who can pick a face which shows what their pain is like.
• Numerical scale – patients pick a number from 0 (no pain) to 10 (the worst pain you can imagine)

Activity 2: Match the numbers to the correct pain scale.
1 = PIPP   2 = Wong-Baker Faces 3 = Numerical Pain scale

Number _____

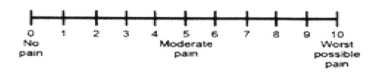

Number _____

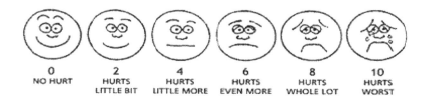

Number _____

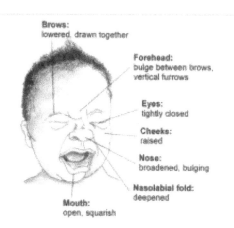

Grammar review: The questions you use to ask about pain

1. Location: Where the pain is?
Where is the pain?
Can you tell me where the pain is?

You will use prepositions like:
in: It's in my hip.
around: It's around my knee.
between: It's between my shoulder blades

You may also use adjectives like:
lower: It's in my lower back.
upper: It's in my upper arm.

2. The type of pain
What's the pain like? – It feels really bad. It's very painful.
What does it feel like? It feels very painful. It hurts a lot.

3. Rating pain on a pain scale
How would you rate your pain on a scale of zero to ten?

4. How long does the pain last?
It comes and goes (the pain is there sometimes but not always)
I have constant pain. (it never stops)

Activity 3: Match the questions about pain with their answers.

1. Can you tell me where the pain is?	a) The pain's really bad.
2. What's the pain like?	b) It's an eight.
3. How bad is the pain?	c) Yes, it aches all the time.
4. How would you rate your pain from zero to ten?	d) It's very painful.
5. Does it hurt all the time?	e) It's in my hip.

Activity 4: Watch the video at www.youtube.com/watch?v=aQYvd6T76og and answer the questions.

1. Why doesn't Mrs Browne feel well?
a)   She has a stomach ache.
b)   Her tooth hurts.
c)   She has a lot of pain.

2. Where is her pain?
a)   In her left hip
b)   In her right knee.
c)   In her right hip.

3. What is her pain like?
a)   It's only a bit painful.
b)   It hurts a little bit.
c)   It hurts a lot.

4. How does Mrs Browne rate her pain on the pain scale?
a) She says it's a five.
b) She says it's a sad face.
c) She says it's an eight.

5. The nurse says she can bring some painkillers because Mrs Browne _____.
a) only had them a few minutes ago.
b) wants them.
c) had some tablets a long time ago.

Types of painkillers.
The medical term for painkillers is 'analgesia'. When you talk to patients you should say 'painkillers'. Analgesia can be given in several ways:

1. tablet – medicine with a hard cover

2 capsule – medicine with a soft cover

3 injection - a sharp object which pushes medicine into the skin

4. suppository – medicine which is put into the rectum and dissolves

5. PCA (Patient Controlled Analgesia) – medicine in a large syringe which is connected to the patient. The patient pushes a button when they want some analgesia

Activity 5: Label the painkillers 1- 5

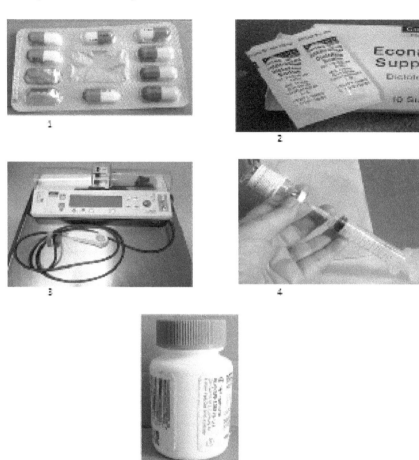

Activity 6: Write a short explanation to a patient about how a PCA works. How will the pain medication be delivered? How does the lock out function work?

Unit 6: Infection Control

Check that you know these terms:
anti-microbial
bacteria
bug / micro-organisms
face mask
germ
gloves
goggles
hand wash / hand gel
hand hygiene / hand washing
isolation
plastic apron
PPE / Personal Protective Equipment
spread of disease
virus, viruses

PPE is an acronym which stands for:
Personal Protective Equipment

Activity 1: Label the pictures below.

hand gel   gloves   face mask

plastic apron   hand washing   goggles

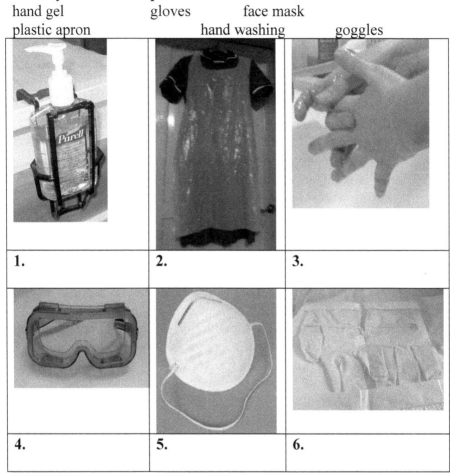

1.	2.	3.
4.	5.	6.

Read the text and then answer the questions that follow.
Infection Control

Infection Control is very important for patient care. Infection Control includes some simple ways which prevent the spread of micro-organisms and disease. Micro-organisms are *'bugs'* or *germs* like bacteria and viruses and can only be seen under a microscope.

One of the ways to stop germs from spreading from one patient to another is by using good hand hygiene. Hand hygiene includes hand washing with soap and water and hand cleansing using antimicrobial hand wash or hand gel. You should clean your hands before and after you do anything with your patients.

Nurses also use PPE or personal protective equipment if they need extra protection from micro-organisms. PPE includes putting on a disposable, plastic apron to cover your uniform, putting on a disposable face mask to avoid breathing in micro-organisms and using disposable gloves. Sometimes nurses wear goggles to stop micro-organisms getting into their eyes.

Activity 2:
1. Infection Control prevents micro-organisms _____.
a from spreading
b growing
c being seen under a microscope

2. The prefix 'micro' e.g. in microscope means _____.
a   very large
b   massive
c   very small

3. Hand hygiene means to _____.
a use disposable gloves
b keep your hands clean
c wash your patient's hands

4. PPE is the term for equipment which ___ nurses from germs.
a takes
b covers
c protects

Activity 3: Complete the text about Infection Control.

hygiene   clean   protection
cover   patient   spread

Infection Control is very important for (1) _____ care.
Infection Control includes some simple ways which prevent the (2)
_____ of micro-organisms and disease. Micro-organisms are
'*bugs*' or *germs* like bacteria and viruses and can only be seen
under a microscope.

One of the ways to stop germs from spreading from one patient to
another is by using good hand (3) _____. Hand hygiene
includes hand washing with soap and water and hand cleansing
using antimicrobial hand wash or hand gel. You should (4) _____
your hands before and after you do anything with your patients.

Nurses also use PPE or personal protective equipment if they need
extra (5)_____ from micro-organisms. PPE includes putting on
a disposable, plastic apron to (6) _____ your uniform, putting on
a disposable face mask to avoid breathing in micro-organisms and
using disposable gloves. Sometimes nurses wear goggles to stop
micro-organisms getting into their eyes.

Activity 4: Watch the video at
www.youtube.com/watch?v=ah2Wj7dtP24.
Put the notes into their correct order.

1. clean hands with hand gel

2. put on disposable mask

3. patient in isolation room

4. put on plastic apron

5. stop infection spreading

Activity 5: Match the beginnings and endings of the sentences.

1. Your father has	a) with the hand gel.
2. He's in an	b) on a plastic apron.
3. Clean your hands	c) a disposable mask.
4. You need to put	d) a serious infection.
5. Put on	e) isolation room at the moment.

Activity 6: Complete the dialogue.

Nurse: Your father has a _____ infection. He's in an isolation room at the moment.

Relative: Oh? Why is he there?

Nurse: We are trying to stop the _____ spreading to the other patients. Or, to his visitors.

Relative: It sounds bad. Is it dangerous?

Nurse: No, it's not dangerous but we have to be careful. I'll just explain what you have to do before you go into the _____ room.

Relative: OK.

Nurse: First, clean your hands with the _____ outside the room.

Relative: All right. Clean our hands. Anything else?

Nurse: Yes. You need to put on a _____. The aprons are also outside the room.

Relative: I see. The white, plastic aprons. OK.

Nurse: Last, put on a disposable _____. Then you are ready to go into the room.

Unit 7: Talking about Conjunctivitis

Check that you know these terms :
conjunctivitis
coating
eye brow
eye lash
eye lid
gauze
inflamed / inflammation
itchy
sterile water
sticky
swollen
to water / watering of the eye
don't touch

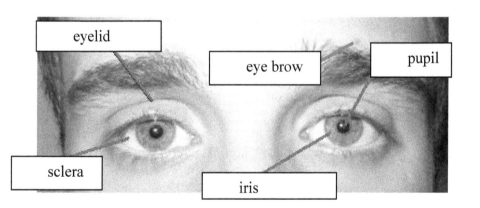

eyelid

eye brow

pupil

sclera

iris

Activity 1: Label the picture of the eye

eye lid   pupil   eyelashes   conjunctiva   eye brow

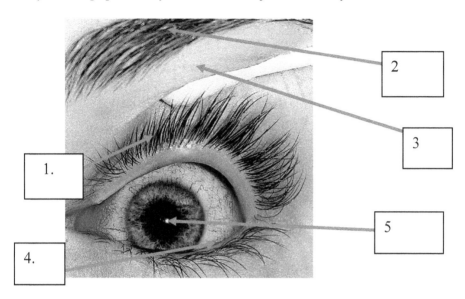

Talking about eye infections
Before you start, review these terms:

inflamed – red and swollen
inflammation - swollen because of infection
coating – fluid which covers a part of the body
itchy – something that is so uncomfortable that you want to rub it
sticky – something which sticks like glue
to water – when liquid leaves the eye

Activity 2: Complete the sentences using the words below.

covering   itchy   inflammation   coating   waters   infection

1. Conjunctivitis means _____ or infection of the conjunctiva.

2. Conjunctivitis is also called 'pink eye' because the eye
_____ makes the eye look red.

3. The conjunctiva is the thin _____ of the front of the eye.

4. In conjunctivitis, there may be a sticky _____ on the eye
lashes.

5. The eye may become very _____ and painful.

6. You may notice that your eye _____ when you have
conjunctivitis.

Grammar: describing symptoms

'It is + adjective' or 'They are + adjective' to describe how
something feels or looks.
For example,
It is painful. / They are painful.   It isn't painful. / They aren't
painful.
It is sore. / They are sore.   It isn't sore. / They aren't sore.
It is itchy. / They are itchy.   It isn't itchy. / They aren't itchy.
It is inflamed. / They are inflamed.   It isn't inflamed. / They aren't
inflamed.

Activity 3: Watch the video and answer the questions that follow. The video is found at
www.youtube.com/watch?v=vJdNJnjJ08A

1. What does the patient tell the nurse? She says that _____.
a. she can't see
b. her eyes are very sore
c. she can't open her eyes.

2. What do the patient's eyes look like? Her eyes are _____.
a. red
b. closed
c. open

3. What do her eyes feel like? They feel _____.
a. itchy and wet
b. cold and painful
c. itchy and painful

4. What will the doctor probably give the patient?
a. eye drops or eye ointment
b. water to clean them
c. sterile drops

5. What does the nurse tell the patient to do?
She tells her to ___ .

a. put some eye drops into her eyes
b. clean her eyes with sterile water and gauze
c . put ointment into her eye with gauze

Activity 4: Match the questions with the answers.

1. Are they sore?   a Yes, they are red.

2. Are they painful?   b Yes, they are itchy.

3. Are your eyes red?   c No, they aren't painful.

4. Are they itchy?   d Yes, they are very sore.

Activity 5: Complete the dialogue by completing the sentences.

Patient: Nurse / can / look at / eyes, please? They / very sore.

Nurse: Sure. Can /open / eyes /look at me?

Patient: Ooh. I can't open / easily.

Nurse: Your eyes / quite red, / they?

Patient: Yes, / are. They / very painful.

Nurse: Are / itchy?

Patient: Yes, / very itchy. And / eyes keep watering all / time.

Nurse: I'll ask / doctor / take / look. He may prescribe / eye drops / eye ointment / you.

Patient: OK.
Nurse: Please try not / touch / eyes. I'll give / some sterile water / gauze / clean them.

Patient: Thank you. I'll try not to touch my eyes at all.

Unit 8: Talking about Depression

Check that you know these terms and expressions:
anti-depressant
depressed
down / down in the dumps
miserable
mood
There's no point to my life
sad
suicide / to commit suicide
to have your ups and downs

Activity 1: Complete the sentences using the words below.
unhappy   mind   sad   sometimes   feel   kill yourself

1 If you feel depressed, you feel very _____ most of the time.

2 A mental illness is an illness which affects your _____ or the way you think.

3 To feel 'down in the dumps' means to feel _____ or miserable.

4 If you say that you have your 'ups and downs' it means that you _____ feel happy and sometimes sad.

5 To commit suicide means to take your own life or to_____.

6 A person's mood is the way they_____. We say a person is 'in a good mood' (happy) or 'in a bad mood' (annoyed).

Read the text and answer the questions that follow.

Depression

Many people find it difficult to talk about depression. They may feel that having a mental illness is a weakness. Or, they may feel that other people will not want anything to do with them if they admit that they have depression.

Some people use expressions other than 'depression' to explain how they feel. They may say that they feel miserable or that they are 'down in the dumps'. Sometimes people may say that they have their 'ups and downs'. This makes it sound as if the way they are feeling is not very serious.

People with depression can feel extremely sad for long time. They may feel that there is no point to their life. They often feel very tired and may say that they are not interested in life. People with severe depression may even try to commit suicide.

Activity 2: Answer the questions about the text.

1. Some people don't want to talk about depression because they think _____.
a people might think they are weak
b people may think they have a serious illness
c people don't want to listen

2. If you say you have your 'ups and downs', it means _____.
a you are depressed all the time
b you are severely depressed
c you feel sad sometimes and happy at other times.

3. Depression is _____.
a feeling unhappy almost all the time
b feeling sad because something bad has happened
c happiness at all times

4. People who are very depressed for a long time may _____.
a take a trip to hospital
b take their own life
c live their life quietly

Grammar Focus : Feel + adjective
We use an adjective after 'feel' to explain how we feel.

For example,

I feel tired / sleepy / exhausted.

I feel sad / depressed / miserable / down.

I feel uninterested in life.

Activity 3: Complete these dialogues below.

Dialogue 1
Nurse: How are you feeling, Julie?
Patient: Not good. I feel _____ all the time.
Nurse: I see. Has anything made you _____?
Patient: No. I just can't stop feeling like this.

Dialogue 2:

Nurse: How are things today?
Patient: I don't know. I don't know how I feel.
Nurse: It's OK. Do you still feel _____-?
Patient: Yes. I feel so tired. There's no _____ at all.

Watch the video and complete the activities that follow.
www.youtube.com/timedtext?v=VDff8YaFTvI&video_referrer=wa
tch&action_view=1

Activity 4: Match the questions with the patient's answers.

1. How are you feeling now?	a) It's been a couple of months now.
2. What is making you feel sad?	b) You mean anti-depressants?
3. How long have you been feeling like this?	c) I still feel sad most of the time.
4. It might be a help to take some tablets for a little while.	d) Maybe I'll do that.
5. It would be a good idea to speak to your GP about it.	e) I don't know. There's just no point to my life.

Grammar Focus: Present Perfect

When we ask **How long?** we use the Present Perfect or the Present Perfect Continuous

Present Perfect = have + past participle e.g. have you lived

Present Perfect Continuous = have been + present participle

e.g. have you been living

The answer uses **'for'** (for a few days / weeks/ years) or **'since'** (since 2010)

For example:

1. How long have you been feeling sad? I've been feeling sad for a few weeks.

2. How long have you been feeling down? I've been feeling down for days.

3. How long have you been feeling depressed? I've been feeling depressed since 2009.

Activity 5: Unjumble the answers to the questions.

1 How does Jane feel now?

Answer: of the time /she feels / sad most

2 What is making Jane sad?

Answer: what / Jane doesn't know / is making her sad

3 How long has Jane been feeling depressed?

Answer: depressed for / a couple of months / she's been feeling

4 What does the nurse think might help Jane?

Answer: Jane / medication / she thinks anti-depressant / might help

5. Who does the nurse think Jane should speak to?

Answer: her GP / be a good idea / she says / to talk to / it would

Unit 9: Talking about Lung Cancer

Check that you know these terms:
bronchoscopy
cancerous
chronic cough
cough up blood
hoarse
CT
lobe
lymph node
mass
medical history
sputum specimen

Activity 1: Match the terms with their correct meanings.

Before you start, review these terms:
-oscopy   a view into the body using a special microscope

1. bronchoscopy	a) another word for tumour
2. cancerous	b) a harsh type of voice
3. mass	c) something which lasts a long time
4. hoarse	d) view into the bronchi or tubes leading from the trachea
5. chronic	e) gland or lump of lymph tissue
6. lymph node	f) cells which contain cancer

Activity 2: Complete the sentences using the terms below.

X-ray   illnesses   lobes   specimen jar   cough up
airways   cancer   long time   lump   harsh

1. A bronchoscopy shows what the inside of the _____ of the lungs look like.

2. A mass is cancerous if it contains _____ cells.

3. A person who has a chronic cough has had the cough for a _____.

4. It is very serious if you _____ blood.

5. A hoarse voice is very _____ and may be a sign of lung cancer.

6. A CT scan is a type of _____ which shows a 3D view of the inside of the body.

7. The lung has several _____ or separate parts.

8. A lymph node is a _____ of lymph tissue which filters the blood.

9. The medical history is a list of _____ and operations a patient has had.

10. Patients cough up sputum into a _____ to be tested for cancer cells.

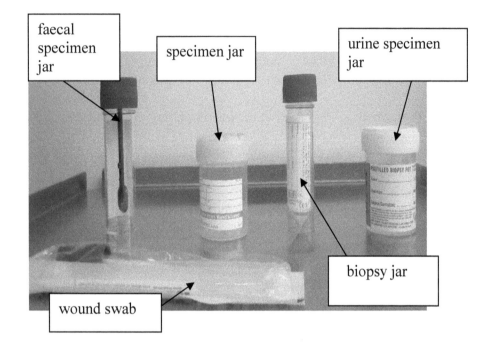

faecal specimen jar

specimen jar

urine specimen jar

biopsy jar

wound swab

Activity 3: Label the picture of the lungs of a person with lung cancer. Use the words below to help you.
The picture is taken from: usana.family.my/files/2013/01/Lung-Cancer.gif
Check that you know the terms.

bronchus   cancerous mass   upper lobe
lobes of the lung   trachea   lymph node

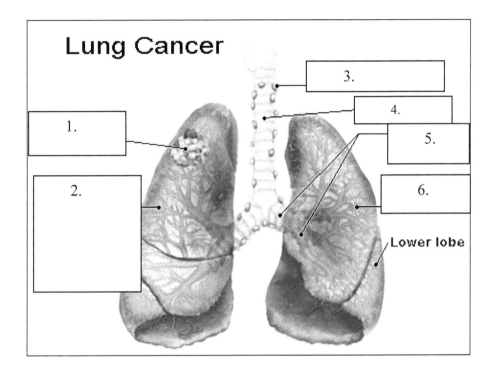

Lung Cancer

1.

2.

3.

4.

5.

6.

Lower lobe

Types of communications: Giving a handover
Nurses have to give each other information about their patients and about patient care. Handovers are also called 'hand offs' (in America). Nurses may give a handover during shift change-over. They explain to nurses on the next shift what care they have given to patients and what care they still need to have.

When patients are first admitted to a ward, nurses give information about the patient's medical history. They also explain what tests or procedures the patient has to have. For example, blood tests and operations.

Activity 4: Watch the youtube video at
www.youtube.com/watch?v=NXb52o8qSTs . Then answer the
questions that follow.

1. Why is Mr Paisit having tests tomorrow?
a for a chest infection
b for lung cancer
c for a cough

2. What is his medical history?
a He is a smoker and has a cough.
b He has asthma and has a cough.
c He has a lot of sputum.

3. What sort of specimen does Mr Paisit have to give the nurse?
a a urine specimen
b a blood sample
c a sputum specimen

4. What sort of test will he have this afternoon?
a an MRI
b a CT scan
c an X-ray

5. Mr Paisit has to be prepared for a _____ the next day.
a a bronchoscopy
b an endoscopy
c a colonoscopy

Activity 5: Match the beginnings and endings of the questions and sentences.

1. Can you tell me about	a) blood?
2. Is he coughing up	b) of his lungs this afternoon.
3. But his doctor asked for	c) a bronchoscopy tomorrow at 8.30.
4. He'll have a CT scan	d) his medical history?
5. He also has an appointment for	e) a sputum specimen for testing.

Activity 6: Put the dialogue in the correct order.
a) Right. I'll make sure that he's ready on time.
b) OK. Can you tell me about his medical history?
c) Mm. So, he needs to give us a sputum specimen. OK.
d) I see. Is he coughing up blood?
e) OK.

Nurse 1: Mr Paisit is having some tests tomorrow to check for lung cancer.

Nurse 2: _____

Nurse 1: Sure. He is a heavy smoker and has a chronic cough. He has also had a hoarse voice for several weeks.

Nurse 2: _____

Nurse 1: No, he isn't. But his doctor asked for a sputum specimen for testing.

Nurse 2: _____

Nurse 1: He'll have a CT scan of his lungs this afternoon.

Nurse 2: _____

Nurse 1: He also has an appointment for a bronchoscopy tomorrow at 8.30.

Nurse 2: _____

Lesson 10: Talking about Dysphagia

Check that you know these terms:
chew
choke
dysphagia
heartburn
liquids
lose weight
manage
pureed
soft food
solid food
Speech and Language Therapist
to swallow
swallowing
thickened fluids
stick to the back of the throat
get stuck

Medical prefixes: 'dys-'
The prefix 'dys-' means 'difficult' of difficulty

There are many terms which use the prefix 'dys-' For example:
dysphagia   difficulty swallowing (-phagia = eat)

dyspnoea (dyspnea US)   difficulty breathing (-pnoea/-pnea = breathing)

dysphasia   difficulty speaking e.g. after a stroke (-phasia = speaking)

Vocabulary:

There are several different words which are used to describe the profession of Speech Pathology'

Speech and Language Therapist (SALT) is used in the UK

Speech Pathologist (SP) in Australia

Speech-Language Pathologist in the USA

Words relating to eating

Activity 1: Match the terms on the left with the correct meanings on the right.

1. chew	a) food which is not liquid
2. swallow	b) burning pain in the chest after eating
3. soft food	c) use the teeth to make food softer in the mouth
4. solid food	d) any fluids which people can drink
5. liquids	e) food which is soft and does not need to be chewed
6. heart burn	f) liquids which are thick enough so a person doesn't choke
7. thickened fluids	g) food which had been mixed together like a thick soup
8. pureed	h) pass food from the mouth to the stomach

Activity 2: Complete the information about chewing and swallowing.

choking   soft food   swallow
chew   stomach   throat

First, food enters the mouth. You (1) _____ the food to

make it into a soft ball called a *bolus* so it is easier to swallow.

Some patients may need to have (2) _____ if they are not able

to chew well e.g. because they have problems with their teeth.

Next, the tongue helps to move food towards the back of the

(3)_____ or pharynx. The food needs to be in small

pieces or it is too difficult to (4) _____ .

Finally, you swallow the food. It moves down the back of the throat

into the oesophagus. The epiglottis, a small flap at the bottom of

the throat, closes over before the food moves towards the

(5) _____ . This is to stop food accidentally going into

the trachea and lungs. This is called (6)_____ or

aspiration.

Activity 3: Label the following pictures.

a) Chew the food
b) Move the food to the back of the throat
c) Swallow the food

(1) _____

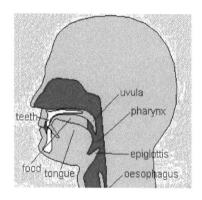

(2) _____

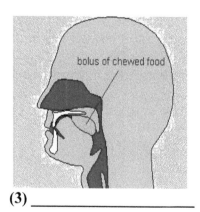

(3) _____

Activity 4: Watch the video at
www.youtube.com/watch?v=qJ8_KsEscJM.
Answer the questions that follow.

1. Mrs Windsor is having difficulty _____.
a eating
b drinking
c swallowing

2. What kind of food can she manage?
a liquids
b soft food
c solid food

3. Mrs Windsor says that when she swallows, it's _____.
a painful
b painless
c uncomfortable

4. Has Mrs Windsor had any weight loss lately?
a No, she still weighs the same.
b Yes, but she's only lost a little bit of weight.
c Yes, she's lost a lot of weight lately.

5. What does the nurse say she'll bring for Mrs Windsor to try?
a free fluids
b thickened fluids
c liquids

Activity 5: Put the notes of the video in the correct order.

1. difficulty swallowing?

2. where food gets stuck?

3. lost weight?

4. check swallow reflex

5. heartburn with dysphagia?

6. bring thickened fluids

7. solids more difficult to swallow than liquids?

Activity 6: Match the beginnings to the ends of the questions.

1. Do you have difficulty	a) get stuck?
2. Is swallowing	b) with the dysphagia?
3. So, it's more difficult	c) lost weight lately?
4. Where does the food	d) swallowing?
5. Do you get any heartburn	e) painful?
6. Have you	f) to swallow solids than liquids?

Activity 7: Complete the dialogue.

Nurse: I'd like to check your _____ reflex, Mrs Windsor. You seem to cough a lot when you are eating.

Patient: Yes, I am having quite a few problems eating at the moment.

Nurse: Do you have difficulty _____?

Patient: Yes. I can only manage soft food.

Nurse: So, it's more difficult to swallow _____ than liquids. Is that right?

Patient: Yes. I can't eat anything which isn't soft. I have a lot of yoghurt and soups.

Nurse: Is swallowing _____?

Patient: Not really painful just uncomfortable. If I don't eat soft food it feels as though it's getting _____ and won't go down. It makes me feel like being sick.

Nurse: That's not very good at all. It must be very unpleasant for you. Where does the food get stuck?

Patient: It seems to get stuck at the back of my _____. I'm not sure how far down it is.

Nurse: OK. Do you get any _____ with the dysphagia?

Patient: No. It just seems to be hard to swallow anything. I can't eat much at all.

Nurse: Have you lost _____ lately?

Patient: Yes, I've lost a lot of weight. Around 6 kilos in a couple of weeks.

Nurse: All right, I see. I'll try you with some liquids in a little while. I'll bring some _____ fluids for you to try to see if you can manage them.

Answers:
1. Blood pressure
Activity 1:
1. blood press - ure
2. pulse
3. nor - mal
4. pain – kill – ers
Activity 2:
1.c She wants to take Mr Browning's blood pressure and pulse.
2.b The patient's blood pressure is a bit high.
3.c The patient's pulse is faster than usual.
4.c The nurse thinks the patient's blood pressure is a bit high because he might be in pain.
5.a The painkillers might make his blood pressure go down.
Activity 3:
Nurse: Hello, Mr Browning. Can I take your blood pressure and pulse, please?
Patient: Oh, hello nurse. Yes sure.
Nurse: Mm. Your blood pressure's a bit faster than this morning. And your pulse is faster than usual.
Patient: Oh, are they? Why is that?
Nurse: If you are in pain, your blood pressure will go up and your pulse will get faster.
Patient: Yes, I'm in quite a bit of pain at the moment.
Nurse: I'll get you some painkillers. Then your blood pressure should go down and your pulse should get slower too.
Patient: I see. Thanks for explaining it to me.
Activity 4: b   f   a   e   c   d
Activity 5: 1.d   2.a   3.e   4.b   5.c
Activity 6
Nurse: Can I take your blood pressure and pulse, please?
Patient: Oh hello, nurse. Yes sure.

Nurse: Your blood pressure's a bit higher than (usual) this morning. Your pulse is faster than usual.

Patient: Oh, are they? Why is that?

Nurse: If you are in pain, your blood pressure will go up and your pulse will get faster.

Patient: Yes, I'm in quite a bit of pain at the moment.

Nurse: I'll get you some painkillers. Then your blood pressure should go down and your pulse should get slower too.

Patient: I see. Thanks for explaining it to me.

Activity 7:
1. take your pulse.
2. do an ECG. (electrocardiogram, EKG)
3. take your temperature.
4. take some blood.
5. do a urine test.

Unit 2. Talking about movement

Activity 1:   1.c   2.f   3.a   4.e   5.b   6.d

Activity 2: 1. lie down   2. sit up   3. stand up
4. stand behind   5. sit down   6. lift up

Activity 3:

1.b Nurse Hannah asks the patient to sit up first?

2.c Next, Nurse Hannah asks the patient to stand up facing her.

3.a The patient says she finds it difficult to walk.

4.b The patient should try not to lean back or she may fall.

5.c The last thing the patient does is to sit down.

Activity 4: (1) **sit up**   **(2) walk**   (3) **lean** (4) **turn** (5) **fall**?

Activity 5: Some suggestions

Pronunciation:

It's much easier to pronounce example (b) because the end of the first word (stand) merges into the beginning of the next word which starts with a vowel (up)

There are a lot of these phrasal verbs in English. Think of them as belonging together:

(a) lean forward, face me

(b) stand up, turn around

a) This one is consonant + consonant - **Can you siT Down, please?**

b) This is consonant + vowel - **Can you stanD Up, please?**

Sounding softer:

If you are giving a command, it sounds softer if you say 'Try to', 'Can you just...' or 'Just..'.

You can also add 'for me' to make a command sound softer: e.g.

Can you sit down for me?

Try to lean forward, Can you just stand up, Just walk towards me.

Of course, if it is an emergency and you want your patient to do something NOW, you use the imperative. e.g. **Turn around! Sit down.**

Giving encouragement

In the dialogue the nurse wants to let the patient know she is doing the right thing so she says:

That's right. She could also say **That's good. You're doing well. Great.**

Unit 3. **Talking about pneumonia**

Activity 1:1. bronchi 2. lung   3. alveoli

Activity 2: 1c   2e   3a   4b   5f   6d

Activity 3: 1. cough 2. sputum 3. sneeze 4. sneezing 5. phlegm

Activity 4: 1. a 2. b   3. b   4.c

Activity 5:

Nurse: How long have you HAD the cough?   (have)

Patient: Oh, I've had it for over a week now. I FEEL awful. (feel)

Nurse: Can you please COUGH into this specimen jar? (cough)

Patient: I'll TRY. (cough cough) There you are! Yuk. It's green. (try)

Nurse I'll giv:e you some oxygen to make it easier to BREATHE. (breathe)

Patient: Thank you. It is difficult.

Nurse: I'll GIVE you some tablets to help with the pain. (give)

Patient: Thank you. My chest HURTS a lot. (hurt)

4: Answers

Just some general points.

Breast reconstruction is making a breast again, usually after a mastectomy. The prefix 're-' means 'again'.

Pronunciation: from lessons 3 and 4

1. Make sure you pronounce the 's' and 't' clearly in these words:

quite   It's quite normal

first   in the first week

scars   the 's' at the end of the word sounds like a 'z'

please   the 's' sounds like a 'z'

easier   it has 3 syllables (word parts) eas – i – er

breathe   difficult sound. Not 'th' e.g. breath. It's a deep sound 'the' breathe. The same sound as the word 'the'.

check   Must be a 'ch' sound e.g. Can I check your wound? Can I check your blood pressure?

wash   This is the 'sh' sound e.g. Can I wash you?

well   Make a round shape with your lips to say the 'w' sound.

Unit 4: Breast reconstruction

Activity 1:

1.   ar – e – <u>**o**</u> - la

2.   <u>breast</u>

3.   <u>com</u> – fort - able

4.   in – <u>fec</u> - tion

5.   <u>nip</u> - ple

6.   <u>numb</u> - ness
7.   re – con –<u>struc</u> - tion
8.   <u>up</u> -right

Activity 2:
1.c chest wall
2.g chest muscle
3.b fat lobules
4.f nipple
5.a areola
6.h milk ducts
7.e fatty tissue
8.d skin

Activity 3: 1. heals 2. scar 3. numb 4. sports bra 5. upright

Activity 4: (c) Is that OK?

Activity 5: 1.b 2.a 3.c numb 4.b 5.c 6.c

Activity 6: 1.d 2.f 3.a 4.e 5.b 6.c

Nurse: Hello, Mrs Song. I'm going to explain what will happen after your breast reconstruction. Is that OK?

Patient: Oh yes. I don't know much about it.

Nurse: After your surgery we'll check your breasts every hour for the first four hours.

Patient: I see. OK.

Nurse: That's to check that your breasts are healing well.

Patient: All right.

Nurse: You may have numbness around your nipples after the surgery. Don't worry. This is quite normal.

Patient: A numb feeling? I didn't know that. How long will it last?

Nurse: It could be for a while, even up to a few months after the operation.

Patient: Oh well. It's good to know that it's normal.

Nurse: Yes, it's quite normal. You need to wear your new sports bra all day for the first week. Then you can just wear it during the day.

Patient: OK. So, wear the bra day and night for the first week.

Nurse: Make sure that you sleep upright during the first week as well.

Patient: Do you mean sleep sitting up in bed?

Nurse: That's right. It will be more comfortable for you too.

Patient: What about scars? I don't want to get any scars on my breasts.

Nurse: You will get exercises which will help with this. One last thing. Watch for any signs of infection in your breasts. Call us if you are worried at all.

Patient: Thank you. I'll do that.

Activity 7: 1e 2.b 3.d   4.c 5.f 6.a

Pronunciation:

worse   nurse   this is a tricky sound. You will see it spelled as 'er','ir','or' and 'ur'

er   certain

ir   third   thirsty

or   worse

ur   purple   nurse   Thursday   hurts

sports - the end sound must be clearly t-s .

Other examples, warts   charts   parts   starts hurts

The 'r' sound

right   write

rate   heart rate pulse rate

respirations

Unit 5: Some difficult words here. Let's look at some of them.

analgesia   I gave her some analgesia an hour ago.

ache   - 'ch' sounds like 'k' because it comes from the Greek language.
Noun: an ache, aches   e.g. I've got a lot of aches. **stomach ache**
verb: to ache e.g. It aches a lot. Be careful to add the 's' to the 3rd person singular (he,she,it)
capsule - listen for the 'sh' sound cap - sule
drug chart – you'll also hear it called a medication chart or meds. chart
to hurt : It hurts a lot
injection
PCA – we often use the acronym when we talk about this e.g. I set up Mrs Smith's PCA and she's using it already.
patient controlled analgesia
pain
I'm in pain.
It's painful
pain scale
painkillers
rate your pain - the 'r' sound is difficult for some of you. It's a good idea to practise the whole question 'How would you rate your pain? And say 'rate' quite slowly.
suppository - notice the pronunciation supp – os –it – (o) ry   (we sort of 'swallow the last 'o') e.g. I gave her a Voltarol supporitory tablet
NSAID - 'en – said' or non-steroidal
Non Steroidal Anti-inflammatory. Another pronunciation note: I say 'anti' as 'antee' (Australian pronunciation) but the US pronunciation is 'antai' – use whichever pronunciation you prefer.
   Activity 1: 1. hurts 2. aches 3. painful   4. stomach ache 5. back pain   6. sharp
   Activity 2:
   3 Numerical (means 'using numbers)

2   Wong Baker Faces (named after the two people who developed the scale)
1   PIPP (an acronym – each letter stands for a word)

Activity 3: 1.e   2.a   3d.   4.b   5.c

Activity 4: 1.c   **2.**c   In her right hip. **3.**c   **4.**c   **5** c

Activity 5: 1.capsules 2. suppositories 3. PCA
4. injection 5. tablets

Dialogue:

Nurse: Hello Mrs Browne. How are you feeling today?

Patient: Not very well.

Nurse: That's no good. What's the problem?

Patient: I've got a lot of pain at the moment.

Nurse: Can you tell me where the pain is?

Patient: Yes. It's in my hip. My right hip. It's aching a lot.

Nurse: (nods her head) OK. I see. Can you tell me what the pain is like? How bad it is.

Patient: Oh it's really bad. Very, very painful.

Nurse: Uh huh. How would you rate your pain on a scale of zero to ten? Zero is no pain and ten is severe pain.

Patient: It's an eight. It's much worse than this morning.

Nurse: Does it hurt all the time?

Patient: Yes it aches all the time. It's worse when I try to walk. Can I have some pain killers, please?

Nurse: Let me check your drug chart. Yes, it's OK. You had some pain killers more than four hours ago. I can get you some now.

Patient: Thanks, nurse. I think I'll go back to bed for a while.

Nurse: All right. I'll be back in a minute with the tablets.

Unit 6: Infection Control
Activity 1: 1. hand gel   2. plastic apron   3. hand washing
4. goggles   5. face mask   6. gloves - sterile and non-sterile gloves
Activity 2: 1.a   2. c   3. b   4.c
Activity 3: 1. patient   2. spread   3. hygiene   4. clean
            5. protection   6. cover
Activity 4:
patient in isolation room
stop infection spreading
clean hands with hand gel
put on plastic apron
put on disposable mask
Activity 5: 1.d   2.e   3.a   4.b   5.c
Activity 6: dialogue
Nurse: Your father has a serious infection. He's in an isolation
room at the moment.
Relative: Oh? Why is he there?
Nurse: We are trying to stop the infection spreading to the other
patients. Or, to his visitors.
Relative: It sounds bad. Is it dangerous?
Nurse: No, it's not dangerous but we have to be careful. I'll just
explain what you have to do before you go into the isolation room.
Relative: OK.
Nurse: First, clean your hands with the hand gel outside the room.
Relative: All right. Clean our hands. Anything else?
Nurse: Yes. You need to put on a plastic apron. The aprons are also
outside the room.
Relative: I see. The white, plastic aprons. OK.
Nurse: Last, put on a disposable mask. Then you are ready to go
into the room.

Unit 7: Conjunctivitis
Notes:
The 'ch' sound – we have some more words now:
check - I'm going to check your wound.
touch - Don't touch your eyes, please.
itchy – My skin is very itchy.
Consonants: Make sure that you pronounce all the consonants:
ointment
gauze
disposable
plastic apron
'tion' sound is 'shun' e.g. infection
'x' sound is 'ks'
explain – 'I'll explain it to you'
expert – He's an expert in the field.
 sterile   means without micro-organisms
e.g.
sterile water for injection(to make up an IV antibiotic) or *sterile water for irrigation (to use in a dressing, to clean the wound)*
sterile field – the area which is clean when you do a dressing
Activity 1: 1.eye lash 2. eye brow 3. eye lid 4. conjunctiva
5.pupil
Activity 2: 1. inflammation   2. infection   3. covering
          4. coating   5. itchy   6. waters
Activity 3:1.b 2.a 3.c 4.a   5.b
Activity 4:   1.d 2.c 3.a   4.b
Activity 5:
Patient: Nurse, can you look at my eyes, please? They're very sore.
Nurse: Sure. Can you open your eyes and look at me?
Patient: Ooh. I can't open them easily.

Nurse: Your eyes are quite red, aren't they?

Patient: Yes, they are. They're very painful.

Nurse: Are they itchy?

Patient: Yes, they're very itchy. And my eyes keep watering all the time.

Nurse: I'll ask the doctor to take a look. He may prescribe some eye drops or eye ointment for you.

Patient: OK.

Nurse: Please try not to touch your eyes. I'll give you some sterile water and gauze to clean them.

Patient: Thank you. I'll try not to touch my eyes at all.

Unit 8 Depression: Answers

Pronunciation:

ups and downs   There are a lot of expressions in English in this format. They are called 'fixed expressions' because they must always be in the same order e.g. *something and something.*

See if you know these ones:

1 black and white e.g. It's all there, in black and white.

2 black and blue e.g. She was beaten black and blue.

3 ins and outs - e.g. She knows all the ins and outs about it.

4 down and out. e.g. Poor man. He's really down and out.

5 out-and-out   e.g. She's an out-and-out liar.

Activity 1: 1. unhappy   2. mind   3. sad

                4. sometimes 5. kill yourself 6. feel

Activity 2: 1a   2c   3a   4b

Activity 3: Dialogue 1

Nurse: How are you feeling, Julie?

Patient: Not good. I feel down all the time.

Nurse: I see. Has anything made you unhappy?

Patient: No. I just can't stop feeling like this.

Dialogue 2:

Nurse: How are things today?
Patient: I don't know. I don't know how I feel.
Nurse: It's OK. Do you still feel depressed?
Patient: Yes. I feel so tired. There's no point to life at all.

Activity 4:
Nurse: Hello, Jane. How are you feeling now?
Patient: Oh I have my ups and downs. I still feel sad most of the time.
Nurse: Uh huh. What is making you feel sad?
Patient: I don't know. There's just no point to my life.
Nurse: How long have you been feeling like this?
Patient: It's been a couple of months now.
Nurse: It might be a help to take some tablets for a little while.
Patient: You mean anti-depressants?
Nurse: Yes. It would be a good idea to speak to your GP about it.
Patient: OK. Maybe I'll do that. I need something, that's for sure.
Activity 5:
1. She feels sad most of the time.
2. Jane doesn't know what is making her sad.
3. She's been feeling depressed for a couple of months.
4 She thinks anti-depressant medication might help Jane.
5. She thinks it would be a good idea to talk to her GP.
Unit 9: Lung Cancer
1. Fixed expressions
1. 1 black and white e.g. It's all there, in black and white. = means that it is written down (the 'white' = paper and the 'black' = ink)
2. black and blue e.g. She was beaten black and blue. = means she has a lots of bruises and she was beaten badly.
3. ins and outs - e.g. She knows all the ins and outs about it. =

She knows all the details.

4. down and out. e.g. Poor man. He's really down and out.= he has no money and no home.

5. out-and-out   e.g. She's an out-and-out liar. = a complete liar.

2. –oscopy always means 'view using a special microscope'. This is a common suffix.

1. colonoscopy   view the colon or large intestine
2. colposcopy   view the cervix
3. endoscopy   view of the internal organs of the body
4. laparoscopy   view into the abdomen

3. Words which mean tumour. Notice that these words do not always mean 'cancer'. This is why people like to use them.

mass   e.g. a mass in his stomach
growth e.g. a growth on his kidney
lump   e.g. a breast lump

Activity 1: 1.d   2f   3a   4.b   5c   6e

Activity 2: 1.airways 2.cancer 3.long time 4.cough up 5.harsh
6. X-ray 7.lobes 8.lump 9.illnesses 10.specimen jar

Activity 3: 1.cancerous mass   2. lobes of the lung   3. lymph node
                4. trachea   5. bronchus   6. upper lobe

Pronunication: These words come from Greek: 'ph' = 'f'
e.g.lymph
'ch' = k trachea, bronchus

Activity 4: 1.b   2.a   3.c   4.b   5.a

Activity 5: 1.d   2.a   3.e   4.b   5.c

Activity 6: the completed dialogue

Nurse 1: Mr Paisit is having some tests tomorrow to check for lung cancer.

Nurse 2: OK. Can you tell me about his medical history?

Nurse 1: Sure. He is a heavy smoker and has a chronic cough. He has also had a hoarse voice for several weeks.

Nurse 2: I see. Is he coughing up blood?

Nurse 1: No, he isn't. But his doctor asked for a sputum specimen for testing.

Nurse 2: Mm. So, he needs to give us a sputum specimen. OK.

Nurse 1: He'll have a CT scan of his lungs this afternoon.

Nurse 2: OK.

Nurse 1: He also has an appointment for a bronchoscopy tomorrow at 8.30.

Nurse 2: Right. I'll make sure that he's ready on time.

Unit 10:dysphagia

1. colonoscopy - view into the colon or intestines – cancer of the colon

2. colposcopy – view into the vagina – cancer of the cervix

3. endoscopy – view into the internal organs through the mouth into the gastrointestinal tract

4. laparoscopy – view into the abdomen – called 'keyhole surgery' or 'minimally invasive surgery'

X-ray – view of bones

CT Scan – 3D view of body organs

MRI scan – detailed view of internal organs

PET - Positron emission tomography – 3D view of processes of the body e.g. image of a tumour

Some pronunciation notes:

1. quite - you must say the 't'

It's quite bad.

It's quite painful.

It's quite uncomfortable.

It's quite sore.

2. liquid - 'lik- wid'

   'qu' sound is 'kw' – it's not common.

   quality

   quantity

liquify - make liquid

3. 'x' sound. 2 sounds:

1. 'ks'   six   mix
2. 'gs'   exit wound

Activity 1: 1.c   2. h   3.e   4.a   5.d   6.b   7.f   8.g

Activity 2: 1.chew 2.soft food 3.throat 4.swallow 5.stomach
6.choking

Activity 3: 1.c   2a   3b

Notice the word **bolus** in the picture?

Activity 4: 1.c   2.b   3.c   4.c   5.b

Activity 5:   4, 1, 7, 2, 5, 3, 6

Activity 6:   1.d   2. e   3.f   4.a   5.b   6.c

Activity 7:

SLT: I'd like to check your swallow reflex, Mrs Windsor. You
seem to cough a lot when you are eating.

Patient: Yes, I am having quite a few problems eating at the
moment.

SLT: Do you have difficulty swallowing?

Patient: Yes. I can only manage soft food.

SLT: So, it's more difficult to swallow solids than liquids. Is that
right?

Patient: Yes. I can't eat anything which isn't soft. I have a lot of
yoghurt and soups.

SLT: Is swallowing painful?

Patient: Not really painful just uncomfortable. If I don't eat soft
food it feels as though it's getting stuck and won't go down. It
makes me feel like being sick.

SLT: That's not very good at all. It must be very unpleasant for
you. Where does the food get stuck?

Patient: It seems to get stuck at the back of my throat. I'm not
sure how far down it is.

SLT: OK. Do you get any heartburn with the dysphagia?

Patient: No. It just seems to be hard to swallow anything. I can't eat much at all.

SLT: Have you lost weight lately?

Patient: Yes, I've lost a lot of weight. Around 6 kilos in a couple of weeks.

SLT: All right, I see. I'll try you with some liquids in a little while. I'll bring some thickened fluids for you to try to see if you can manage them.

Lightning Source UK Ltd.
Milton Keynes UK
UKHW020705050619

343870UK00006B/1274/P